WITHDRAWN

W9-AIL-344

WEEKLY WR READER®
EARLY LEARNING LIBRARY

INVENTORS AND THEIR DISCOVERIES

George Eastman
and the Camera

by Monica L. Rausch

Reading consultant: Susan Nations, M.Ed.,
author/literacy coach/consultant
in literacy development

Science and curriculum consultant:
Debra Voege, M.A., science and math curriculum
resource teacher

Please visit our web site at: www.garethstevens.com
For a free color catalog describing Weekly Reader® Early Learning Library's list
of high-quality books, call 1-877-445-5824 (USA) or 1-800-387-3178 (Canada).
Weekly Reader® Early Learning Library's fax: (414) 336-0164.

Library of Congress Cataloging-in-Publication Data

Rausch, Monica.
    George Eastman and the camera / by Monica L. Rausch.
       p. cm. — (Inventors and their discoveries)
    Includes bibliographical references and index.
    ISBN-13: 978-0-8368-7499-0 (lib. bdg.)
    ISBN-13: 978-0-8368-7730-4 (softcover)
    1. Eastman, George, 1854-1932—Juvenile literature. 2. Photographic industry—United States—Biography—
Juvenile literature. 3. Inventors—United States—Biography—Juvenile literature. I. Title.
TR140.E3R38   2007
770.92—dc22   2006029996

This edition first published in 2007 by
Weekly Reader® Early Learning Library
A Member of the WRC Media Family of Companies
330 West Olive Street, Suite 100
Milwaukee, WI 53212 USA

Copyright © 2007 by Weekly Reader® Early Learning Library

Editor: Dorothy L. Gibbs
Cover design and page layout: Kami Strunsee
Picture research: Sabrina Crewe

Picture credits: cover (main), pp. 4, 8, 11, 18 © Paul Almasy/Corbis; cover (right), title page, p. 7 Library of
Congress; p. 5 The Granger Collection, New York; pp. 6, 9, 13, 14, 15 © Bettmann/Corbis; pp. 10, 16, 17, 20, 21
© North Wind Picture Archives; p. 12 Science Museum/Science and Society Picture Library.

All rights reserved. No part of this book may be reproduced, stored in a retrieval
system, or transmitted in any form or by any means, electronic, mechanical,
photocopying, recording, or otherwise, without the prior written permission of
the copyright holder.

Printed in the United States of America

1 2 3 4 5 6 7 8 9 10 10 09 08 07 06

FAIRFIELD CHILDREN'S LIBRARY
1080 Old Post Road
Fairfield, CT 06824

Table of Contents

Chapter 1: Say "Cheese!" 4

Chapter 2: The Man Behind the Camera 8

Chapter 3: From Wet to Dry 11

Chapter 4: The Kodak Moment 18

Glossary 22

Books 23

Web Sites 23

Index 24

Cover: In 1888, George Eastman made an easy-to-use camera (left). It was small enough for people to hold in their hands. In 1895, he made a much smaller camera (right) that was even easier to use.

Cover and title page: George Eastman (1854–1932) made photography easy for everyone.

Chapter 1
Say "Cheese!"

Click! Click! Snap! Somebody was taking pictures.
It was May 1888. People were taking lots of pictures!
They were using handheld **cameras** made by the
Eastman Dry Plate and **Film** Company.

Everyone was excited. The cameras were so easy to use! People did not need to know much about **photography**. They did not have to work with messy **chemicals**. They did not have to know how to print their pictures on paper. "Just push the button, and we do the rest!" George Eastman told people.

Before Eastman invented his handheld camera, most pictures of people were taken in special rooms called studios. Only people called photographers took pictures.

The film was inside the camera. When people wanted to print their pictures, they just sent their cameras to Eastman's company. The company printed the pictures on paper, filled the cameras with new film, and sent them back.

People could take picture after picture with Eastman's camera — without stopping! The film inside the camera could hold as many as one hundred pictures.

film

The pictures taken with Eastman's first handheld camera came out round when they were printed.

Eastman had invented a new kind of film and a new way to take pictures. With more and more cameras around, the world seemed like a new place. People had to be careful about what they did on the streets. Someone could — CLICK — snap a picture!

Chapter 2
The Man Behind the Camera

George Eastman was born on July 12, 1854, in Waterville, New York. His father died when Eastman was only seven years old. At age thirteen, Eastman had to leave school and get a job. He had to make money to help his mother and his older sisters.

Eastman's first job was in an office. The job did not pay Eastman very much money, but he learned a lot about business while he worked. In 1874, he started working at a bank. The bank job paid him a lot more money.

At age thirteen, George Eastman worked as a messenger boy for an insurance company. The job paid him three dollars a week.

After four years, Eastman had saved enough money for a trip. A friend told him to carry a camera with him on the trip so he could take pictures. Eastman bought a camera, but he never took the trip. He decided to study photography instead!

Taking pictures away from a studio was not easy. A photographer had to carry along a kit of liquid chemicals and glass plates. The photographer also needed to find a dark place nearby to print the pictures.

© North Wind Picture Archive

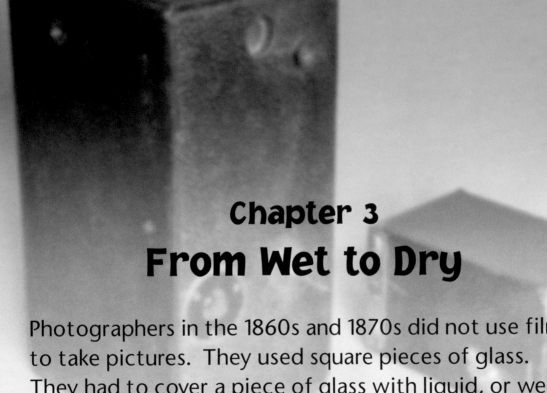

Chapter 3
From Wet to Dry

Photographers in the 1860s and 1870s did not use film to take pictures. They used square pieces of glass. They had to cover a piece of glass with liquid, or wet, chemicals before putting it in a camera. After taking pictures, they had to make paper prints very quickly, before the chemicals on the glass plates dried.

Richard L. Maddox was a doctor in England. His idea to use dry chemicals to make photographs meant that photographers would not have to print the pictures right away.

In 1871, Richard L. Maddox invented a way to use dry chemicals to make photographs. Eastman wanted to learn about this new way to take pictures. He thought that if the glass plates used dry chemicals, the plates could be made in factories and sent to photographers. Eastman believed that dry glass plates would make taking photographs much easier.

For three years, Eastman worked on making his own dry plates. He also worked on a way to make the plates quickly and easily. In 1880, he invented a machine that made his dry plates.

The chemicals on dry plates were not a dry powder. They were a gelatin, or jellylike, material. A machine could spread the gelatin more evenly on glass plates than by hand, so pictures from machine-made plates were less blurry.

Eastman started selling his dry plates to photographers right away. The photographers were excited. They bought lots and lots of Eastman's plates. After about a year, Eastman founded a company that sold the plates.

Eastman started The Eastman Dry Plate Company in 1881. In 1882, the company moved into this building in Rochester, New York. In 1884, the name of the company changed to The Eastman Dry Plate and Film Company.

Even using dry plates, photographers still had a lot to carry around. They needed lots of glass plates. They also needed special holders for the plates to help keep them from breaking.

Although his dry plates were a big success, Eastman was not satisfied. Photographers could take only one to four pictures on each plate so they needed many plates to take many pictures. The glass plates were difficult to carry around. They were also fragile, or easily broken.

Eastman wanted to put the chemicals for taking pictures on another kind of material. He wanted to use material that was not as heavy as glass and could bend without breaking. In 1885, Eastman invented film that was flexible. He put the chemicals on paper instead of on glass.

Eastman's flexible paper film could be rolled up. Eastman and one of his workers, William Hall Walker, invented special rollers for the film. The film was stretched from one roller to another inside the camera.

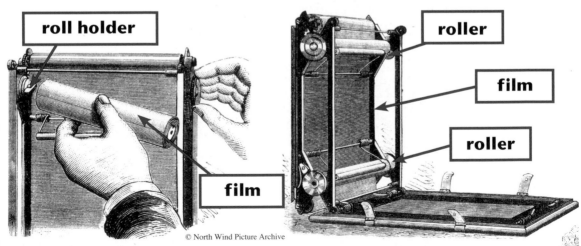

roll holder

roller

film

roller

film

© North Wind Picture Archive

The film was on a roll inside the camera. Now photographers could take many pictures very quickly, one after another. After taking one picture, the photographer just rolled the film forward. Then the camera was ready to take another picture. There were no glass plates and no messy, wet chemicals.

Eastman and Walker made a box that could be put on the backs of cameras. The box covered the film.

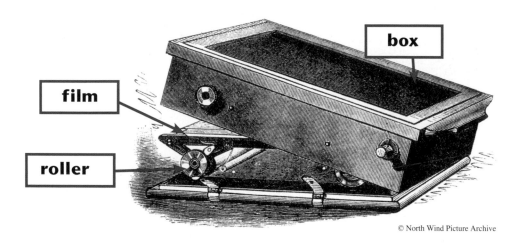

box

film

roller

© North Wind Picture Archive

Chapter 4
The Kodak Moment

Eastman still was not finished! He had made film that was easy to use, but he wanted to make a camera that was easy to use, too. In 1888, Eastman invented a small camera that he could hold in his hands. He called the camera "the Kodak."

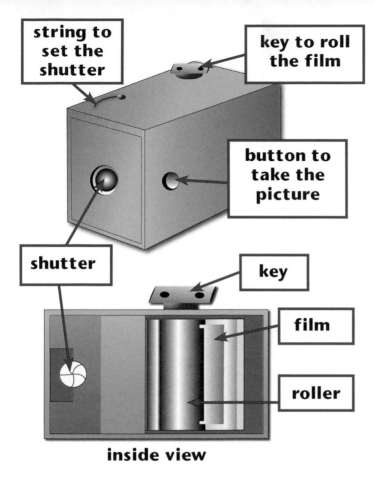

string to set the shutter

key to roll the film

button to take the picture

shutter

key

film

roller

inside view

Taking a picture with the Kodak camera was very easy. A person had to follow only three steps: 1) Pull a string to set the **shutter** in place. 2) Push a button to open the shutter and take the picture. 3) Roll the film forward to take another picture. Anyone could do it!

The shutter opens to let light into the camera. When the light hits the film, it changes the chemicals on the film to make the picture.

In May 1888, a person could buy a Kodak camera for twenty-five dollars. After filling the film with pictures, the person just sent the camera to Kodak. For ten dollars, Kodak printed the pictures, put new film in the camera, and sent it back.

In the 1890s, when people sent their cameras to Eastman's company, women in a rooftop workroom "did the rest." They made prints of photographs by holding the film from the cameras in sunlight.

© North Wind Picture Archive

People no longer needed photographers to take pictures. They no longer had to go to studios. They could take pictures of anything, anywhere, all by themselves. Everyone wanted George Eastman's Kodak camera!

Eastman's company sold a lot of Kodak cameras, and George Eastman became a very rich man. During his life, he gave more than $100 million to universities, hospitals, and music schools.

© North Wind Picture Archive

Glossary

chemicals — materials that scientists called chemists work with and study

film — a thin sheet of material covered with chemicals that change to form a picture when they are hit by light

flexible — able to bend easily without breaking

fragile — easy to break or harm

gelatin — a jellylike substance, or material

insurance — the business of selling agreements to protect the value of people or property

invented — found a new way of doing something or made a new tool for doing a task

photographers — people who take pictures with cameras

photographs — pictures taken with cameras and captured on the film inside the cameras

photography — the science of taking and printing photographs

shutter — the part of a camera that opens to let light hit the film and then closes again to keep light away from the film

studios — rooms that are set up for taking photographs

Books

Click! A Book about Cameras and Taking Pictures. Gail Gibbons
(Scholastic)

George Eastman: The Kodak Camera Man. Famous Inventors (series).
Carin T. Ford (Enslow Elementary)

Taking Pictures. Greg Lang (Sundance)

Web Sites

George Eastman
library.thinkquest.org/J002039F/george_eastman.htm
Learn about George Eastman's life and his inventions and have
fun finding the special message hidden in an Eastman puzzle.

The First Snapshots
photomuse.org/EXHIBITIONS/FIRSTSNAPSHOTS/images.html
See pictures taken in 1888 to 1895 with Eastman's Kodak cameras.

Publisher's note to educators and parents: Our editors have carefully
reviewed these Web sites to ensure that they are suitable for children. Many
Web sites change frequently, however, and we cannot guarantee that a site's
future contents will continue to meet our high standards of quality and
educational value. Be advised that children should be closely supervised
whenever they access the Internet.

Index

chemicals 5, 10, 11, 12, 13, 16, 17, 19

Eastman Dry Plate and Film Company 4, 6, 14, 20, 21

film 6, 7, 11, 16, 17, 18, 19, 20

film rollers 16, 17, 19

Kodak cameras 18, 19, 20, 21

Maddox, Richard L. 12

photographers 5, 10, 11, 12, 14, 15, 17, 21

photographs 12, 20

photography 5, 10

plates, dry 12, 13, 14, 15

plates, glass 10, 11, 12, 13, 15, 17

printing pictures 5, 6, 7, 10, 11, 12, 20

shutters 19

studios 5, 10, 21

Walker, William Hall 16, 17

About the Author

Monica L. Rausch has a master's degree in creative writing from the University of Wisconsin-Milwaukee, where she is currently teaching composition, literature, and creative writing. Monica likes to write fiction, but she says sticking to the facts is fun, too. Monica lives in Milwaukee near her six nieces and nephews, to whom she loves to read books.